Hardened heart
The greed of man

Andrew L. Ritchie

Copyright © 2012 by Andrew L. Ritchie

Hardened Heart
by Andrew L. Ritchie

Printed in the United States of America

ISBN 9781624195440

All rights reserved solely by the author. The author guarantees all contents are original and do not infringe upon the legal rights of any other person or work. No part of this book may be reproduced in any form without the permission of the author. The views expressed in this book are not necessarily those of the publisher.

Unless otherwise indicated, Bible quotations are taken from the New King James Version of the Bible. Copyright © 2007 by Thomas Nelson, Inc.

www.xulonpress.com

Table of Contents

Part I

<u>Man's Hardened Heart</u>

Introduction	vii
The Chosen People	11
Pursuit of Wealth, where does it lead	35
Corruption of the Church	43
Martyrdom for Christianity	54
Heart of a Servant	71
Heart of the Church	75
Conclusion	95
References	99

Introduction

Not long ago God put a message on my heart to discuss in depth mankind's hardened heart, and how we have become consumed by our own greed, and throughout my life how I have been greedy with a hardened heart.

Before we go any further, what is a hardened heart? In simplest terms it's when your heart becomes hard to others and you only think of yourself.

For most of my adult life that is how my heart was. It wasn't always hard. Only when I chose to follow my path for my self-worth it was hard, but when I chose to follow God my heart was unhardened. My heart was hardened not only to society, but also to the Lord. Luke 8:5:11-15

"Now the parable is this: the seed is the word of God. Those by the wayside are the ones who hear; then the devil comes and takes away the word out of their hearts, lest they should believe and be saved. But the ones on the rocks are those who, when they hear, receive the word with joy; and these have no root, who believe for awhile and in time of temptation fall away. Now the ones that fell among thorns are those who, when they have heard, go out and are choked with cares, riches and pleasures of life, and bring no fruit to maturity. But the one that fell on the good ground are those who, having heard the word with a noble and good heart, keep it and bear fruit with patience."

In essence Jesus was referring to how the Word was received by man's heart. If you take a look at western society, over the past fifty years we have entered into a post-Christianity era. In many lives today God is not the focus, but money and self is. For a very long time that is how my heart was. The seed for me was in the thorns. Where is your heart today?

Broken down on the side of the road struggling with a flat tire, motorists driving past me at highway speed honking their horns, the thoughts going through my mind "Why doesn't someone stop and help?" Sound familiar? Well I was also the motorist speeding by and honking. Have you ever driven by a homeless person, only to roll up the window when they approach? Have you ever changed the television channel when you see a commercial for hungry children? If you are like me, then you have. But don't feel bad you are not alone. Mankind has been doing it since the beginning with Adam and Eve and we haven't stopped.

As everyone knows in the beginning there was Adam and Eve. The Garden of Eden was a wondrous place filled with trees laden with fruit. In the midst of the garden was a tree with fruit on it, which God had commanded you shall not touch it or eat it lest you die (Gen3: 2-3).

And the woman said to the serpent, "we may eat the fruit of the trees of the garden; but of the fruit of the tree which is in the midst of the garden, God has said you shall not eat it, nor shall you touch it lest you die."

The serpent coerced Eve into eating of the fruit by saying *"You will not surely die, For God knows that in the day you eat of it your eyes will be opened, and you will be like God knowing good and evil."* Gen. 3:5

When Adam and Eve ate the fruit, they began the journey that man has not been able to avoid the greed of man. Right from the beginning mankind has been on a headlong journey of self- gratification. Never happy with what we have, always trying to get better, regardless of the outcome.

The chosen People

Ever since God's covenant with Abraham, Gen. 15:18 on the same day the Lord made a covenant with Abram, saying "to your descendents I have given this Land from the river of Egypt to the great river, the river Euphrates."

In modern terms God gave from the brook of Egypt to the Euphrates. This is roughly from Port Said in Egypt to the Euphrates in modern day Iraq. Could this have been the Garden of Eden? Only God knows.

God's covenant with Abraham began a journey for the Israelites, which still goes on today. As you will see, it has not been an easy journey, but at times the path that God lays before us, is not an easy path.

In the 1990's Sir Andrew Lloyd Webber, brought back to Broadway an amazing production called

"Joseph and the Technicolor Dream Coat" starring Donny Osmond. It is a show based on the Bible story of Joseph and the tunic of many colors.

According to the Bible here is a man, who was hated by his brothers, eventually sold to the Egyptians and rose to second only to the pharaoh.

Genesis 37:3-4

Now Israel loved Joseph more than all his children, because he was the son of his old age. Also he made him a tunic of many colors. But when his brothers saw that their father loved him more than all his brothers, they hated him and could not speak peaceably to him.

I have a question for you; can you honestly sit there and say that you have never hated or resented your brother? If you answered no I have never resented or hated my brother then you're a hypocrite, because the only one who never resented or hated his brother is Jesus Christ. Some of you may be saying "I don't have a brother", or "I only have sisters". In the biological sense that may be true, but in God's eyes we are ALL brothers and sisters. In my own struggles, I have resented my brothers, both biological and my brothers in God's eyes.

My brother was a better swimmer, better in school, had an easier time getting dates. But even through my resentment my brother was and is always there for me. Through his compassion I eventually learned that my petty jealousy was just that, petty. He got everything first because he was older than me, but that it didn't mean he was any better than me just different and older. Now how did I feel about my spiritual brother?

Before I turned my life over to God, I was a very hateful, resentful man. I loathed those who were more successful than me, and I always tried to go after jobs not for the desire of the job, but for the money and prestige that went with it. I was consumed by titles. I worked hard to get the golden egg. Did I get it? No! I was too busy showing off by saying to friends "Want to go out tonight, I'm buying" and when the money was gone so were the friends.

Through my 20's and 30's especially, if someone had offered me a Ferrari for my brother, outwardly I would have said no, but inwardly it would have been YES. I was no different from Joseph's brothers. Have you ever resented the brother at work, who got the promotion and raise over you? Outwardly it would be congratulations, inwardly why wasn't it me? If you look deep inside that is how it would be.

How did Joseph react to being thrown in a pit and sold to the Egyptians?

Joseph was sold to the Egyptians when he was seventeen

Genesis 39:1

Now Joseph had been taken down to Egypt. And Potiphar, an officer of Pharaoh, captain of the guard, an Egyptian, bought him from the Ishmaelites who had taken him down there.

The captain found favor with Joseph and made him the overseer of his house. The master's wife found Joseph to be handsome in form and appearance. She tried to get Joseph to lie with her, Joseph relented. Eventually the master's wife caught Joseph by his garment and again tried to get him to lie with her, Joseph fled leaving his garment in her hand. The master's wife kept the garment and showed it to the master when he returned home. The master's anger was aroused and had Joseph arrested and taken to the King's Prison.

Here is a man who was concerned for his brothers,

but his brothers resented him and took his tunic of many colors. They plotted to kill him, but instead threw him in a pit with no food and water, sold him, and eventually he ended up in prison because of what they had done to him.

If I was in Joseph's shoes, I think my initial reaction would be complete disbelief in what had just happened. Some of you would probably say kill them, but would you really? My biggest feeling is sorrow, for his brothers, that they could be that insecure in themselves to plot to kill their own flesh. Joseph's brothers are a very good example of when you take your focus off of God and put your focus on possessions. Later on in history another man was tortured and crucified. Our Lord Jesus Christ, how did he react? Luke 23:34

Then Jesus said" Father, forgive them, for they do not know what they do."

In the 20th century when Pope John Paul II was shot, he prayed for forgiveness of the shooter.

According to the Bible, Joseph was eventually released from prison, became second to the pharaoh, and put in charge of rationing of the grain and livestock during the famine that overcame Egypt and Canaan.

Genesis 42:2

When Jacob saw that there was grain in Egypt, Jacob said to his sons "Why do you look at one another?" And he said "Indeed I have heard that there is grain in Egypt; go down to that place and buy for us there, that we may live and not die"

The brothers remembered that they had sold Joseph, what they didn't know is that the overseer that they would be dealing with was their brother. According to the Bible, Joseph recognized his brothers, but because Joseph now had the look of an Egyptian, they didn't know they were dealing with Joseph.

Joseph dealt harshly with his brothers, he accused them of being spies, and his brothers confirmed for him that there were 12 of them from one man in Canaan. He kept them in prison for three days, and then sent them to get the youngest brother and Simeon stayed back. Without his brothers knowledge Joseph filled their bags with grain and had their silver placed in the bags as well.

The brothers returned with Benjamin, the youngest, to Egypt where Joseph had them brought to his house. His brothers were scared because when

The Chosen People

they had returned to Canaan they discovered that the silver had been returned to them. When they came back to Egypt they had the original silver plus more silver to be able to buy more grain, Joseph had a noon meal with his brothers and fed Benjamin more than the rest.

In the morning Joseph commanded his servant to fill the bags with grain, place the silver in the bags, and in Benjamin's bag he had placed a silver cup. After his brothers left Joseph had his brothers followed and when they were beyond the walls had them stopped and searched. When the silver cup was discovered, the brothers were returned to Joseph's house. Joseph wanted to have Benjamin as a slave for having the silver cup in his bag, but his brothers pleaded with Joseph.

Finally Joseph couldn't take anymore and revealed his identity to his brothers. Joseph had played a trick on them; however, Joseph explained to his brothers that God had sent him to Egypt to preserve life. He sent his brothers back to Canaan to get their father and all their families where they would dwell in the land of Goshen.

With Joseph bringing his brothers and their families to Egypt, it would take 430 years before the

Israelites could leave and return to Canaan. It would not be a pleasant part of their history. In the ancient world we have been given the ability to see many wonders that still exist today.

One of these wonders is the Pyramids of Giza. The pyramids were designed by the Egyptians, but were built by the Israelites. For 284 years the Israelites were slaves, who were tortured, beaten, starved, and killed. This happened because the Egyptians were scared that the Israelites were multiplying and fruitful and could lead them to form alliances with Egypt's enemies and fight against them.

The whole time that the Israelites were enslaved, God was with them, they multiplied and were fruitful, which made the Egyptians angrier. Eventually the pharaoh issued a decree.

Exodus 1:22

So Pharaoh commanded all his people saying" Every son who is born you shall cast into the river, and every daughter you shall save alive"

It was during this time that Moses was born, his mother hid him for three months, when she could hide him no longer, she placed him in an ark and then put the ark in the river. A daughter of the Pharaoh found him and raised him as her own. Moses eventually found out he was an Israelite (Hebrew) and when he saw an Egyptian beating on his brethren, he killed the Egyptian and hid him in the sand. When Moses killed the overseer he was trying to protect his brethren. If you look into your heart could you do the same for your brethren?

When I was younger, like a lot of young men, I served my country. For me it was in peacetime, but even then I was still being trained to defend my country. If I was put into a situation where I had to sacrifice my life for my country, would I? Being a Scottish highlander, who have sacrificed countless lives for freedom of the Scottish people; it is a very easy answer for me: Yes!!!

Please take a moment to pray with me for all the men and women of the armed services who have or are putting their lives in harm's way for our freedom.

So that he wasn't put to death by the Pharaoh Moses fled to Midian. Years later when he was tending the flock for his father-in-law the Lord appeared to him in the flame of a burning bush and told Moses:

Hardened Heart: The Greed of Man

Exodus 3:5-6

Then He said "do not draw near this place. Take your sandals off your feet, for the place where you stand is holy ground." Moreover he said "I am the God of your father, the God of Abraham, the God of Isaac and the God of Jacob."

God commanded Moses to return to Egypt and bring His people out and bring them to the land of milk and honey. Moses was being put into a position that he had never before done. God was taking him out of where he was comfortable into a task that he didn't feel he was suited for. Has God done the same to you?

In my own situation, if anyone had come to me a year ago and asked me to write a book, I would have laughed and said I wasn't capable of writing a book. But God has placed this book on my heart, and He is confident that I will glorify Him in writing it. He has other tasks for me and when I am ready, He will guide me through those tasks as well.

After the plagues that struck the Egyptians, Moses led the Hebrews out of Egypt toward the promised land of milk and honey. As they traveled obstacles were placed before them. The first major obstacle was the Red Sea. At the Red Sea, the people complained to Moses.

Exodus 14:12

Is this not the word we told you in Egypt, saying let us alone that we may serve the Egyptians? For it would have been better to serve the Egyptians than that we should die in the wilderness."

Have you ever been in a situation where you thought that God had left you and He brought something unprecedented into your life? About 2 years ago I was following my path, not really paying any attention to God, when disaster struck. I was diagnosed with glaucoma in both eyes. I screamed at God saying WHY ME?? WHAT HAVE I DONE TO DESERVE THIS?? You have probably heard the expression hit rock bottom, to me in those days I went through rock bottom to find a new level of despair.

Depression hit hard and fast and it wasn't long before thoughts of taking my life was a constant companion. This may sound funny, but the thing that was keeping me from taking my life was the thought that kept going through my head that I was born in Scotland and that was where I would leave this world and go to our home in heaven. I prayed to God for forgiveness for how I had initially blamed God for this. God answered me very quickly and said to me "Don't worry I got this.

" On Sunday January 15th 2012, it is probably the most important day of my life I was sitting listening to the sermon and our pastor was teaching from Matthew and one verse it seemed as it was directed at me

Mathew 20:16

"So the last will be first and the first last. For many are called but few chosen."

It was at that time that I really focused on turning my life completely over to God. Two weeks later I had my semi-annual checkup for the glaucoma. When you are dealing with something as horrendous as glaucoma, there is always worry associated with test results. The results were not what I expected. I was told that there was no sign of glaucoma in either eye. I was in shock! The entire drive home I praised God for the miraculous work He is doing in this life that is His. Glaucoma was my affliction with others it could be hepatitis, cancer, alcoholism, or drug addiction with the same results as I had. God has taught me that He gives us these afflictions to bring us closer to Him and He has a task for us where we need to be stronger in our faith to accomplish it. God does answer all prayers but sometimes it's not the answer we expect or the time frame that we expect, but He does answer all prayers.

When the Hebrews were faced with the obstacle of the Red Sea, they turned to Moses to solve the problem of getting across it with the Egyptian armies bearing down on them. They believed in the miracles that God had provided, because they had witnessed them. They didn't believe that they would survive. When they called out to Moses for help they believed that Moses would save them. If they had put their trust in a man, where was their faith?

When God had brought the plagues to Egypt, the Hebrews believed in God. Did their hearts have faith in God, or more importantly how strong was their faith?

To answer this we turn to Luke 9:23

Then He said to them all, "If anyone desires to come after Me. Let him deny himself, and take up his cross daily and follow Me."

Jesus took up our cross, which is our sin, and did so because of His love for us. What this verse says is for us to love Him as best as we can, and give Him our sin, so that we may one day be in His presence eternally.

We have taken for granted the miracles that God bestows on us daily. Simple things like witnessing a sunrise or how about the air we breathe. I have come across many people who have been bitter about the days they have been having and said to them if you woke up this morning how could you be having a bad day? We put so much stock in our worldly possessions that we forget the only possession worth having is God's love.

Before we continue the journey of the Israelites we need to define faith and belief. Belief is the action that is a direct result of faith. Faith is putting our trust and love in God. What I have discovered is that there are three types of faith, which can be referred to as true faith, crisis faith and finally, no faith. No faith is the easiest to describe, churches are full of people today with little or no faith. They are the ones that go to church on Sunday; go through the traditions associated with a church service, outwardly they appear to be followers of God, but inwardly they are counting the minutes till the service is over because they have something better to do. The second group has crisis faith. Crisis faith is a Christian who believes that by the simple act of going to church during a crisis will cause them to be saved. On September 11th 2001 the United States was rocked by the senseless destruction of the World Trade Center in New York City. One of the outcomes of the attack was the alarming amount of people that went to church. For the next several weeks churches were full. People were thinking the end of days were upon us, and by going to church they would be saved. Once the crisis was over, many of those with crisis faith reverted back to their previous lifestyle until the next crisis, where they would return to God.

If you take a look at faith today the last group is unfortunately the smallest group, they are the ones who have true faith. True faith is putting all of your trust and love in God. Regardless of the situation people with true faith, live their lives for God and with God. God places challenges before true believers, but these have been placed before us so that we constantly put our lives in God's hands and let Him have control. I sadly admit that for a good part of my life I was probably somewhere in the middle between crisis faith and little or no faith. But now I am firmly in the true faith group, where God is leading me through life. Which group are you in?

The journey through the wilderness brought the Israelites to Mt. Sinai. The Lord warned the people not to come up Mt. Sinai or touch it, or they would die. Moses spent forty days and nights upon Mt. Sinai. While Moses was on the mountain, the Israelites constructed a golden calf to worship to. They were afraid and reverted to something that they were comfortable with. While being in captivity in Egypt they had been taught to worship gold statues.

Have you ever done something out of fear that you shouldn't have done? Many years ago out of fear for bad decisions I had made, I left my family. It was many years later before I returned or even had contact with them. While I was out of the picture my dad had several heart attacks, I could have lost him and I never would have known. I am so blessed to be able to talk with him and learn from his wisdom that I had taken for granted. My dad wasn't the only one I had been taking for granted, I was also taking God for granted. Have you ever taken God for granted?

We have all heard the expression that power corrupts; the media is full of business leaders and politicians who are examples of this. But this is not a new concept. If you look at ancient Israel you can see the same thing in Saul, David and Solomon. These were three men chosen by God to lead Israel, and at different times, went astray.

Saul was the first king of Israel, when the people cried out for a king; they didn't consider God as king; they wanted their own king. Saul a Benjamite was selected. Initially he was a very humble king, but when king Agag was placed into their hands by God, Saul spared him. Because of this action Saul fell out of favor with God.

1 Samuel 15:7-9

And Saul attacked the Amalekites from Havilah all the way to Shur, which is east of Egypt. He also took Agag king of the Amalekites alive, and utterly destroyed all the people with the edge of the sword. But Saul and the people spared Agag and the best of the sheep, the oxen, the fatlings, the lambs and all that was good, and were unwilling to utterly destroy them. But everything despised and worthless, that they were utterly destroyed.

Have you ever been in a similar position, where you have been told to throw everything away, kept the good stuff for yourself and thrown away the items that were despised or you thought was worthless?

The Star of David flies majestically over the buildings of Israel, as a symbol of one of the greatest kings that Israel ever saw. Samuel was sent to Bethlehem by God to one of Jesse's sons. God instructed Samuel to have all of the sons go before him. It wasn't the way the son's looked on the outside, but how pure their hearts were. None of sons that went before them had an acceptable heart, but not all the sons were there. The youngest was in the pasture tending the flock. When David was brought before Samuel, he was anointed.

1Samuel 16:13

Then Samuel took the horn of oil and anointed him in the midst of his brothers; and the Spirit of the Lord came upon David from that day forward. So Samuel arose and went to Ramah.

During the battle with the Philistines, they had

The Chosen People

a champion who stood nine feet nine inches tall. David approached the champion with a bag of five smooth rocks and a sling. David triumphed over the Philistine.

1Samuel 17:49-51

Then David put his hand in his bag, and took out a stone; and he slung it and struck the Philistine in his forehead, so that the stone sank into his forehead and he fell on his face to the earth. So David prevailed over the Philistine with a sling and a stone, and struck the Philistine and killed him. But there was no sword in the hand of David. Therefore David ran and stood over the Philistine, took his sword and drew it out of his sheath and killed him, and cut his head off with it.

Saul came to resent David, because the people loved David more than they did him. David, as a good and faithful servant to God, willingly did the tasks that Saul asked of him. Eventually David reigned over all of Israel, because during the time of Saul, David had protected Israel from her enemies. Throughout his life, David tried to abide by God's covenant. But like all men he did stumble several times. David gazed upon a beautiful woman bathing who was the wife of Uriah the Hittite.

2 Samuel 11:14-15

In the morning it happened that David wrote a letter to Joab and sent it by the hand of Uriah. And he wrote in the letter saying "Set Uriah in the forefront of the hottest battle and retreat from him, that he may be struck down and die."

David took Uriah's wife, Bathsheba, as his wife and they had a son Solomon. After David passed away Solomon became king of Israel.

David had told Solomon how to build the Lord's temple in Jerusalem. It took a total of 11 years to build the temple: four years to build the foundation and seven years to build the temple. Solomon was very loyal to the Lord and followed God with a solid determination; however, he turned away from God and because of his great love for a multitude of women who followed other gods Solomon built a high place for Chemosh the abomination of Moab.

1 Kings 11:9-11

So the Lord became angry with Solomon, because his heart had turned from the Lord God of Israel, who had appeared to him twice, and had commanded him concerning this thing, that he should not go after other gods; but he did not keep what the Lord had commanded. Therefore the Lord said to Solomon, "Because you have done this, and have not kept My covenant and My statutes, which I have commanded you, "I will surely tear the kingdom away from you and give it to your servant.

In 70 A.D during the Roman Occupation the temple in Jerusalem was destroyed.

Luke 21:5

Then as some spoke of the temple, how it was adorned with beautiful stones and donations, He said "These things which you see- the days will come in which not one stone shall be left upon another that shall not be thrown down."

1942 years later the stones are still in the same place at the bottom of Temple Mount in Jerusalem.

With the destruction of the temple the Jewish people scattered all over the world.

Ezekiel 7:18

They will also be girded with sackcloth; Horror will cover them; shame on every face, baldness on all their heads.

Little would be heard about the chosen people until the 1930's when an Austrian, Adolf Hitler, came to power in Germany. When he was younger, as a poor artist in Vienna, he began to resent the wealth that the Jewish people had. When he came to power, he began passing laws in Germany that limited the wealth that the Jewish people had. Rapidly they lost wealth and positions. When the Second World War began, he began creating concentration camps in the occupied countries. One of the infamous camps was Auschwitz in Poland. Between 1939 and 1945 an estimated six million Jews died under the hands of Nazi Germany.

The average German knew of the atrocities that were happening to the Jews, but from fear for their own lives, few Germans tried to do anything about it. But one man, a factory owner, did what he could to help them. His name was Oskar Schindler; by the end of the war he had saved 1300 lives through bribery, black marketeering and lying.

Under United Nations decree in May of 1948, the nation state of Israel was re-established. But it hasn't been easy for them, as an island of Christian beliefs surrounded by Arab nation's which are predominantly Muslim. Israel has constantly been trying to uphold their sovereignty, and they still do today.

This chapter has been a comprehensive study of the Israelites and how they were treated throughout history. Unfortunately their story isn't unique; their story is an example of how we all treat each other. If you talk to any person, anyone could recount a time in their history where they were abused or put to death for their beliefs, color, race or sex.

At some point in our lives we have all treated our brothers and sisters differently. Before I started following God, I shamefully admit that I treated my brothers and sisters poorly. I was a coward; I could never say anything that was remotely racist or sexist publically, but inside my heart was hardened to their struggles. I have come to realize, that my struggle with different people was shallow and insensitive;

when I eventually realized that we are all children of God and that we are all created in His image, my eyes and heart were opened. Through God's eyes we are all the same, I am trying to live up to that as well. How about you?

Pursuit of Wealth, where does it lead?

When I was 28 I collapsed at work and rushed to the hospital. It was thought that I'd had a heart attack. At that time of my life, I was obsessed with chasing the false idol of money. During that time I was working five jobs working roughly 22 hrs a day. I had been living on coffee and cigarettes.

Where did it get me? I had to take time off work to recover from exhaustion, so I was no further ahead. It wasn't till much later in my life, that I stopped chasing the almighty buck, and finally realized that the whole time I should have been following the Lord. The whole time I hadn't paid attention to God but, He definitely paid attention to me. It would be wonderful to say that the situation I put myself through was unique, but unfortunately it isn't. I had been greedy and self-serving. I felt I could do everything on my own. Sound familiar? Most of you reading this have probably been in similar circumstances.

In the last century the world has been turned upside down by economic turmoil. The 1920's, also known as the roaring twenties, was a decade of carefree living. After the First World War people needed to rebound, people were investing heavily in the 20's trying to get their nest egg bigger with a carefree attitude. But then it happened, the unthinkable: October 29th 1929. The stock market crashed, millions of dollars were lost in a single day, fortunes were lost, plants closed, economies throughout the world came to a screeching halt.

This was only the first thing to happen, after the stock market crashed, major dust storms throughout the Midwest caused farmers to lose their crops. The United States didn't fully recovery from the great depression until after Pearl Harbor was bombed on Dec 7 1941 and the U.S entered the Second World War.

Since the end of the Second World War in the United States there have been 12 economic recessions. In 2007 the world entered what is being called the global financial crisis, which some economists are calling as bad as the Great Depression of the 30's. National banks are being rescued by governments; large manufacturing companies are being rescued.

Personal Bankruptcy is at staggering levels; home foreclosures are at mind-numbing levels. Global spending is out of control. One of the biggest problems is credit cards and online shopping. With online shopping I am just as guilty as anyone, online shopping is fast and easy, don't have to worry about lineups. However, when I do online shopping I use prepaid gift cards, so that when I reach the limit I am done. The average consumer today carries between 6 to 10 credit cards with a monthly balance. Society has become consumed with wealth.

Less than 50 years ago, society had a strong belief in God, people would worship regularly, families were happy, and the church was the center of every community. There were economic troubles back then as well, but personal bankruptcy and home foreclosures were rare. Something happened and society's focus changed from being on God, to focusing on money and what can I do for myself.

If you look at history, when man focused on himself, the end result was never a good thing.

Genesis 6:5-7

Then the Lord saw that the wickedness of man was great in the earth, and the thoughts of his heart was only evil continually. And the Lord was sorry that He had made man on the earth and He was grieved in His heart. So the Lord said "I will destroy man whom I have created from the face of the earth, both man and beast, creeping thing and birds of the air, for I am sorry that I have made them."

End result of man's evil heart was the great flood.

Exodus 33:1

Then the Lord said to Moses, "Depart and go up from here, you and the people whom you have brought out of the land of Egypt, to the land which I swore to Abraham, Isaac and Jacob, saying to your descendents I will give it".

Because of their complaining about food, water and worshipping a golden calf, they spent 40 years in the wilderness and were denied the land of milk and honey.

Luke 21:24

"And they will fall by the edge of the sword, and be led away captive into all nations. And Jerusalem will be trampled by Gentiles until the times of the Gentiles are fulfilled.

Because of the greed in their hearts Israel vanished for 1900 years.

When it comes to wealth the best way to describe wealth is how Jesus Christ, explained wealth to the disciples in the book of Matthew.

Matt.6:19-34

"Do not lay up for yourselves treasures on earth, where moth and rust destroy and where thieves break in and steal; but lay up for yourselves treasures in heaven, where neither moth nor rust destroys and where thieves don't break in and steal. For where your treasure is, there your heart will be also. The lamp of the body is the eye. If therefore your eye is good, your whole body will be full of light. But if your eye is bad, your whole body will be full of darkness. If therefore the light that is in you is darkness, how great is that darkness! No one can serve two masters; for either he will hate the one and love the other, or else he will be loyal to the one and despise the other. You cannot serve God and mammon (wealth).

Therefore I say to you, do not worry about your life, what you will eat or what you will drink; nor about your body what you will put on. Is not life more than food and the body more than clothing? Look at the birds of the air, for they neither sow nor reap nor gather into barns; yet your heavenly Father feeds them. Are you not of more value than they? Which of you by worrying can add one more cubit to his stature?

So why do you worry about clothing? Consider the lilies of the field, how they grow; they neither toil nor spin; and yet I say to you that even Solomon in all his glory was not arrayed like one of these. Now if God so clothes the grass of the field, which today is, and tomorrow is thrown into the oven, will He not much more clothe you, O you of little faith?

Therefore do not worry, saying, what shall we eat? Or what shall we drink? Or what shall we wear? For after all these things the Gentiles seek. For your heavenly Father knows that you need all of these things. But seek first the kingdom of God and His righteousness and all these things shall be added to you. Therefore do not worry about tomorrow, for tomorrow will worry about its own things. Sufficient for the day is its own trouble.

The pursuit of money doesn't get us any closer to heaven; it actually puts us further away. On April 15th 1912, the RMS Titanic sunk in the north Atlantic after hitting an iceberg. The ship was believed to be unsinkable. Benjamin Guggenheim, a wealthy American businessman, was a passenger on board who perished in the frigid north Atlantic waters. What did his wealth do for him that day?

I grew up for part of my childhood in a poor fishing village in northern Scotland. Money wasn't a big concern for most families in the village because nobody had any. We were happy with what we had, laughed and played like most kids do. We went to church on Sunday, where I would run my cars across the water pipes. But we believed strongly in God and prayed every night.

Somewhere along the line, like society, I took my focus off of God and started chasing money. For me personally chasing money wasn't a good choice, but it was a choice I made when I didn't bother to listen to God. I wonder sometimes what my life would have been like if I hadn't desired money so much. But then I realize that God had my path laid out long before I was born. He knew the path that I would follow and the decisions I would make, but He also knew when I would stop chasing worldly pleasures, and follow Him.

It took me a long time to come to the realization that I have all the wealth of the cosmos at my fingertips, and all I had to do was drop to my knees and pray to God for forgiveness for the sins I have committed and believe that God is my Lord and savior. But here is a secret: it is available to every man, woman and child, all you have to do is ask for it. The wealth I am referring to is God's love.

Matthew 7:7-8

"Ask and it will be given to you; seek and you will find; knock and it will be opened to you. For everyone who asks receives, and he who seeks finds, and to him that knocks it will be opened."

Corruption of the Church

What do you think about when you hear corruption of the church?

Do you think about financial corruption? Or do you think of the corruption of the message of the church? Let's take a look at both so that we can understand what church corruption is all about. Corruption of the church is not a 21st century concept, that magically appeared, but it has been around since the beginning of churches. Before we can delve into corruption we need to understand what a church is. According to Webster's dictionary, church can be defined as a building for public and especially Christian worship. It can also be defined as the whole body of Christians. For our purposes here we will be looking at the first definition of church.

There are two types of corruption of the church that need to be addressed: the financial corruption of the church and the spiritual corruption of the church. Each one of these is equally important to the study of corruption of the church.

In Matthew 21:12-13 Then Jesus went into the temple of God and drove out all those who bought and sold in the temple and overturned the tables of the money changers and the seats of those who sold doves. And He said to them, "It is written, My house shall be called a house of prayer but you have made it a den of thieves."

In recent years the entire Christian world has been rocked by law suits in churches, corrupt church leaders, and embezzlement. Church leaders have gone to jail for tax evasion not to mention the senseless waste of parishioners tithing to build bigger more elaborate buildings of worship. In the Old Testament God told how He wanted his tabernacle built and what He wanted it made of. How did we go from cloth walls to marble? Is it so we can say to our brothers and sisters "I pray in a beautiful marble church don't you pray in a rundown building that's over 100 years old?" Mankind keeps trying to outdo each other.

As the Bible teaches us all men are created equal under God. Are these buildings for the grace of God or for the betterment of man? The churches do an incredible job with what they have, if it wasn't for the church a lot of communities wouldn't have the ability to feed the hungry. Let's not forget the missions that churches support, bringing the love of God to those that have never heard of God before. It is dark times that we live in; a time when church leaders have armed security units and travel in bulletproof vehicles so that they won't be harmed.

Throughout world history church leaders or holy men have been an integral part of society. In early Greek and Egyptian societies, the church leaders, or holy men, would advise kings, pharaohs, emperors or leaders on a variety of issues ranging from social problems to expansion through armed conflict. The national leaders would follow the advice of the holy men.

Churches would be the center of the community, where followers would go to worship and for fellowship. What has happened where society conformed to the church? Nowadays the church conforms to society and look at what has happened.

In the early part of the 16th century King Henry VIII of England asked the pope for a divorce from Catherine of Aragon; the king was displeased because Catherine of Aragon was unable to give him a male heir.

Matt. 19:3-6

The Pharisees also came to Him, testing Him and saying to Him, "Is it lawful for a man to divorce his wife for just any reason?" And He answered and said to them " Have you not read that He who made them at the beginning, made them male and female, and said, For this reason a man shall leave his father and mother and be joined to his wife, and the two shall become one flesh? So then they are no longer two but one flesh. Therefore what God has joined together, let no man separate."

Because of the reply that the king received from the pope, he felt compelled to go against the church, the Bible and God, and started the Church of England, which is the present day Anglican or Episcopal Church.

When the church was founded, it was founded on the doctrine of sharing the Word of God, as it was taught to the disciples by our Lord and Savior Jesus Christ. Somehow changes started to take place, where the Word was lost and replaced by traditions of man. Each church today is heavily inundated with tradition. In one church, that is consistently praying to saints. This church feels they are not worthy to pray to our Lord and Savior, however Jesus describes prayer in Matt. 6:5-7

"And when you pray you shall not be like the hypocrites. For they love to pray standing in the synagogues and on the corners of the streets, that they may be seen by men. Assuredly I say to you, they have their reward. But you, when you pray, go into your room, and when you have shut your door, pray to your Father who is in the secret place; and your Father who sees in secret will reward you openly. And when you pray, do not use vain repetitions as the heathen do. For they think they will be heard for their many words."

In the 4th century the act of praying to saints was condemned by the hierarchy of the church, however the act of praying to saints still goes on today. Not only do they pray to the disciples, but they also pray to Mary, the earthly mother of Jesus Christ.

Πάτερ ἡμῶν ὁ ἐν τοῖς οὐρανοῖς·

ἁγιασθήτω τὸ ὄνομά σου·

ἐλθέτω ἡ βασιλεία σου·

γενηθήτω τὸ θέλημά σου,·

ὡς ἐν οὐρανῷ καὶ ἐπὶ γῆς·

τὸν ἄρτον ἡμῶν τὸν ἐπιούσιον δὸς ἡμῖν σήμερον·

καὶ ἄφες ἡμῖν τὰ ὀφειλήματα ἡμῶν,

ὡς καὶ ἡμεῖς ἀφήκαμεν τοῖς ὀφειλέταις ἡμῶν·

καὶ μὴ εἰσενέγκῃς ἡμᾶς εἰς πειρασμόν,

ἀλλὰ ῥῦσαι ἡμᾶς ἀπὸ τοῦ πονηροῦ.

> Original Lord's Prayer in Greek
> as it was found in Mat 6:9

"In this manner, therefore pray:
Our Father in Heaven,
Hallowed be your name.
Your kingdom come,
Your will be done
On earth as it is in heaven.
Give us this day our daily bread.
And forgive us our debts,
As we forgive our debtors.
And do not lead us into temptation,
But deliver us from the evil one.

For Yours is the kingdom and
The power and glory forever amen.

According to the NKJV Bible this is how our Lord and Savior gave it to the disciples. Man feels compelled to change it or not use it at all. Here is a modern version of the Lord's Prayer that I recently found.

The Lord's Prayer(modern version)
Our Father in heaven
Reveal who You are
Set the world right:;
Do what's best as above so below.
Keep us alive with three square meals.
Keep us forgiven with you and forgiving others
Keep us safe from ourselves and the devil.
You're in charge!
You can do anything you want!
You're ablaze in beauty!
Yes. Yes .Yes.

Here in the United States we are blessed with freedom of expression under the Bill of Rights. The group that is responsible for this version of the

Lord's Prayer... would they choose to change the Bill of Rights, U.S Constitution, or the Magna Carta to suit their own needs? Where is the church in these interpretations of the Lord's Prayer? Mankind desperately needs the church to intervene. More importantly we need Jesus to intervene.

The Bible is the written word of God. It tells us how to live in God's love and the circumstances of what will happen when we have failed to live up to the laws that God has decreed. Some churches have brought it upon themselves to change the Bible to suit their doctrine, where as they should be changing their doctrine to conform to the Bible. A very good example of the greed of man, in these instances, is it is obvious that it is about self gratification instead of praising God with His creation.

Over the years I have travelled extensively. I have met people from all walks of life. When it comes to church corruption, there is one thing that shines like a beacon in the darkness: the animosity between various church groups. They believe that the path to salvation is through only their church. The hatred between believers is rampant; the devil's handy work can be readily seen.

We have all heard the term believer, but what actually is a believer? A believer is someone who openly and whole heartedly gives themselves to our Lord and Savior Jesus Christ.

Luke. 9:23

Then He said to them all "If anyone desires to come after Me, let him deny himself, and take up his cross daily, and follow Me

There are so many "believers" that are outwardly showing compassion for their brothers and sisters, but inwardly condemning the person that just cut them off as they were turning into the church parking lot. They seem to have forgotten Matt. 5:39

"But I tell you not to resist an evil person. But whoever slaps you on your right cheek, turn the other to him also."

Then there are the "believers" that have shown up at church hung over, and reeking of alcohol. I sadly admit that before I truly followed God, that was me. I have also come across ministers in that same condition. What kind of example is that to the flock if the minister is reeking of alcohol?

Eph 5:18

And do not be drunk with wine, in which is dissipation; but be filled with the Spirit.

I have briefly touched on the Lord's Prayer and praying to saints. Throughout time churches have taught the physical action of prayer by church doctrine, but does the average believer know how to pray spiritually? Prayer is a way of communicating with God. As kids we were taught by our parents to say nightly prayers. As adults we pray to God to save us from ourselves. God does want to help us; He doesn't want us hurting as all fathers should do with their kids. But how many believers pray to God daily, thanking Him for the glorious creation He has made, and how He gave His only Son so that we one day may glorify in His presence.

I recently came across a statistic, which is absolutely appalling. The average Christian prays 60 seconds per day. In a 24 hr day which has 86400 seconds that translates to .07 % of your day is given to God. And Christians wonder why they don't know how to pray. When as Christians the Holy Spirit empowers us with gifts for our use to spread the word and Love of God to others. These gifts help us to enrich our lives and the lives of others.

The only way to obtain these gifts is through prayer. In my own life prior to fully receiving the love of God, sixty seconds a day would have been a stretch for me. I was so wrapped up in earthly pleasures that I didn't give any of my day to God. I felt very alone. After I gave myself completely to God and began praying several times a day, the changes that occurred daily were and are absolutely phenomenal. God as a great Father has so much to teach us, but the only way to receive His teachings is in prayer. Please join me in prayer to our Almighty God and Glorify in His love as I do daily.

Martyrdom for Christianity

*I*t is with deepest humility that as we delve further into the greed of man, that we now turn our attention to the martyrdom for Christianity.

Throughout time there is one, who prominently stands out for selflessly giving of physical life for others: Our Lord Jesus Christ. Our Lord and Savior was betrayed by one of his disciples, Judas for thirty pieces of silver.

Matt 26:20-25

When evening had come, He sat down with the twelve. Now as they were eating, He said "assuredly I say to you, one of you will betray Me."And they were exceedingly sorrowful and each of them began to say to Him, "Lord is it I?" He answered and said, "He who dipped his hand with Me in the dish will betray Me. The Son of Man indeed goes just as it is written of Him, but woe to that man by whom the Son of Man is betrayed! It would have been good for that man if he had not been born."

Then Judas, who was betraying Him, answered and said "Rabbi is it I?" He said to him, "You have said it."

According to scripture, Judas returned the silver pieces to the chief priest, in hopes that the priest would release Jesus in exchange for the silver. As we know Jesus was crucified and Judas was so distraught that he hung himself.

Prior to the crucifixion Jesus said to the disciples in Matt. 26:31-35

The Jesus said to them, "All of you will be made to stumble because of Me this night, for it is written:

I will strike the Shepherd and the sheep of the flock will be scattered, But after I have been raised I will go before you to Galilee." Peter answered and said to Him, "Even if all are made to stumble because of You, I will never be made to stumble. Jesus said to him," Assuredly I say to you that this night, before the rooster crows, you will deny Me three times." Peter said to Him" Even if I have to die with You, I will not deny You!

The Crucifixion
John 19:17-37

And He, bearing His cross, went out to a place called the Place of a Skull which is called in Hebrew Golgotha, where they crucified Him, and two others with Him, one on either side, and Jesus in the center. Now Pilate wrote a title and put it on the cross. And the writing was:

JESUS OF NAZARETH
THE KING OF THE JEWS

Then many of the Jews read this title, for the place where Jesus was crucified was near the city; and it was written in Hebrew, Greek and Latin.

Therefore the chief priests of the Jews said to Pilate, "Do not write The King of the Jews, but He said I am the King of the Jews."

Pilate answered "what I have written, I have written."

Then the soldiers, when they had crucified Jesus, took His garments and made four parts, to each soldier a part, and also the tunic. Now the tunic was without seam, woven from the top in one piece.

They said among themselves "let us not tear it, but cast lots for it, whose it shall be," that the Scripture might be fulfilled which says:

"They divided My garments among them, and for my clothing they have cast lots."

Therefore the soldiers did these things.

Now there stood by the cross of Jesus His mother, and His mother's sister, Mary, the wife of Clopas, and Mary Magdalene. When Jesus therefore saw His mother and the disciple whom He loved standing by, He said to His mother "woman behold your son! Then he said to the disciple, "Behold your mother!"

And from that hour that disciple took her to his own home. After this, Jesus knowing that all things were now accomplished, that the Scriptures might be fulfilled; said" I thirst!"Now a vessel full of sour wine was sitting there; they filled a sponge with sour wine put it on hyssop, and put it in His mouth. So when Jesus had received the sour wine, He said "it is finished!"And bowing His head, He gave up His spirit. Therefore, because it was the Preparation day, that the bodies should not remain on the cross on the Sabbath (for the Sabbath was a high day), the Jews asked Pilate that their legs might be broken, and that they might be taken away. Then the soldiers came and broke the legs of the first and of the other who was crucified with Him. But when they came to Jesus and saw that he was already dead, they did not break His legs. But one of the soldiers pierced His side with a spear and immediately blood and water came out. And he who has seen has testified, and his testimony is true; and he knows that he is telling the truth, so that you may believe. For these things were done that the Scriptures should be fulfilled," Not one of His bones shall be broken."

And again another Scripture says "They shall look on Him whom they pierced."

After Jesus Christ was arrested, the disciples did flee and Peter did deny the Lord three times before the rooster crowed. Is the will of the flesh stronger than the will of the heart? These were great men who spent three years with the Lord in person, and when they were confronted with death they chose the path of self salvation. To them the preservation of the physical body outweighed the love in their hearts. Their Love of our Lord and God was undeniable. Out of the original twelve disciples, 10 were put to death for their beliefs in our Lord and the holy Word.

In Matt 10: 2:4 Now the names of the twelve disciples are these: first Simon, who is called Peter, and

Andrew his brother; James the son of Zebedee, and John the brother; Philip and Bartholomew; Thomas and Matthew the tax collector; James the son of Alphaeus, and Lebbaeus (Jude) whose surname was Thaddeus; Simon the Cananite and Judas Iscariot, who also betrayed Him.

Peter was crucified in Rome; he begged to not be crucified as the Lord was, because he felt he was not worthy. He was crucified upside down.

Andrew was crucified in Patrae, as Peter had said he didn't feel worthy to be crucified as the Lord had. He was tied to an X-shaped cross, where it is believed that he preached for two days before he succumbed.

Paul. He was originally one of the Pharisees charged with rounding up the disciples. On the road between Jerusalem and Damascus the Lord appeared to him. He was converted and went on to write at least 13 of the epistles. He was beheaded in Rome.

Matthew. It is not known by church scholars exactly how Matthew died, but they believe he was a martyr in Ethiopia.

James the Elder. It is recorded in Acts. 12:1-2

Now about that time Herod the king stretched out his hand to harass some from the church. Then he killed James the brother of John with the sword.

James is the only disciple mentioned in the New Testament as being put to death. He is the first disciple to be made a martyr of for the gospel.

James the Lesser. He was created the first bishop of Jerusalem after Jesus was crucified. From the wall of the temple he was asked by the high priest to deny Jesus. He praised Jesus instead, and was thrown off the wall. He didn't die from the fall, so the public proceeded to stone him. He didn't die from the stoning, so a man was brought forward who proceeded to beat James with the club. James was beaten to death with a club.

Bartholomew. The manner of his death, said to have occurred at Albanopolis in Armenia is equally uncertain; according to some, he was beheaded, according to others, flayed alive and crucified, head downward, by order of Astyages, for having converted his brother, Polymius, King of Armenia

Mathias. He was chosen by vote by the eleven remaining disciples to replace the spot left vacant by Judas. It is believed that during the vote a holy light shone on Mathias. This seems to be an early predecessor of papal elections. He did that which he preached, he made the blind to see and healed the sick men, and he raised the dead men, and did great miracles in the name of Jesus Christ. He was firm in the love of God, and clean of his body, and wise in speaking of all the questions of scripture, and when he preached the word of God many believed in Jesus Christ by his predication. The Jews took him and brought him to justice and had gotten two false witnesses against him to accuse him, then which cast on him first stones, and the other after, and so was stoned, and he prayed that the stones might be buried that the false witnesses had cast upon him, for to bear witness against them that stoned him, and finally he was slain with an axe.

John. He wrote the fourth Gospel, and three Epistles, and the Book of Revelation is also attributed to him. Brought to Rome, tradition relates that he was by order of Emperor Dometian cast into a cauldron of boiling oil but came forth unhurt and was banished to the island of Pathmos for a year. He lived to an extreme old age, surviving all his fellow apostles, and died at Ephesus about the year 100.

Timothy. Timothy wasn't one of the original disciples but where Paul wrote two epistles to him that he be included. Timothy was taken under Nero of the provost of Rome, and was grievously beaten, and had quicklime (a white caustic powder that may have caused the ulcer that Paul referred to in 1 Tim. 5:23) put in his throat and upon his wounds. He was released from prison and went on to become the bishop of Ephesus. That under the emperor Nerva, in the year 97, Timothy was slain with stones and clubs, by the heathens, while he was endeavoring to oppose their idolatrous ceremonies on one of their festivals called Catagogia, kept on the 22nd of January, on which the idolaters walked in troops, every one carrying in one hand an idol, and in the other a club.

Philip. He was crucified according to tradition in Greece, for not worshipping the god of mars, and instead proclaiming Jesus Christ. He was crucified upside down by Emperor Domitian in Hierapolis.

Thomas. Was also known as doubting Thomas, he didn't believe that the resurrected Jesus Christ was Jesus, until Jesus allowed him to stick his hand in the gash on Jesus' body. He was run through with a spear type weapon because he wouldn't worship a false idol.

Simon and Jude. They were two of the original twelve disciples chosen by Jesus Christ. After the ascension they frequently travelled together preaching the Gospel. They were both killed in

Persia. It is believed that Jude was axed and Simon was sawed to death.

John the Baptist.
Mathew 14:3-12

For Herod had laid hold of John and bound him, and put him in prison for the sake of Herodias, his Brother Philip's wife. Because John had said to him "It is not lawful for you to have her." And although he wanted to put him to death, he feared the multitude because they counted him as a prophet. But when Herod's birthday was celebrated, the daughter of Herodias danced before them and pleased Herod. Therefore he promised with an oath to give her whatever she might ask. So she, having been prompted by her mother said, "Give me John the Baptist's head on a platter."

And the king was sorry; nevertheless, because of those who sat with him, he commanded it to be given to her. So he sent and had John beheaded in the prison. And his head was brought on a platter and given to the girl, and she brought it to her mother. Then the disciples came and took away the body and buried it, and went and told Jesus.

Hardened Heart: The Greed of Man

Pope John Paul II

The late spring afternoon was as beautiful as only Rome can make them. It was Wednesday, 13 May 1981, and the Polish Pope, elected less than three years earlier, was on his way to his regular weekly public audience, being driven in his white - and then unarmored - popemobile, through a crowd of 20,000 worshippers. It was a routine occasion, yet imbued with the excitement created by this Pontiff, who was already transforming the way the world saw his office. Suddenly, at 5.17pm, shots rang out. Two bullets struck John Paul II in the stomach. The Pope slumped back, blood staining his white cassock. For an instant, there was only silence. But disbelief turned to horror, then panic. Cries rang out: "Hanno sparato il Papa! Hanno sparato il Papa! [They've shot the Pope]". A minute later, police grabbed a man fleeing from the square. He was a young Turk named Mehmet Ali Agca - and one of the 20th century's great mysteries had begun. A letter found in Agca's pocket did little to elucidate matters. "I, Agca, have killed the Pope so that the world may know of the thousands of victims of imperialism," it said. In the event, of course, John Paul II was not killed and, after a five-hour operation, went on to make a full recovery. It is believed that during the ride to the hospital the pope was praying for forgiveness for the man that had just shot him.

In the dense jungle of central Africa over the top of the regular jungle sounds, you hear the unmistakable sound of men singing: Singing praise songs to our Father Almighty. They are undergoing an extensive training program sponsored and ran by pastors from Far Reaching Ministries an American Christian organization.

Since before the exodus of the Israelites, Africa has been engaged in war and it hasn't stopped. What once was a beautiful lush jungle that reached to the vastness of the Sahara Desert has been ravaged by war. Man's greed and worshipping the false idol of money has driven the African economy for centuries from slave trading for cotton plantations, to gold and diamond mines and oil drilling. A quarter of OPEC member countries are in Africa.

In recent years many African countries such as Uganda, Libya, Somalia and Egypt, to name a few, have been engaged in countless civil wars, with mostly political but also religious, as most of Africa is Muslim. For centuries the African continent has been engaged in Jihad (holy war) between Muslims and Christians.

Most of us have heard that famous quote from the 19th century " Dr. Livingstone I presume". This was a quote from H.M Stanley. Years before a young Scotsman named David Livingstone had gone to hear an address by a celebrated missionary. After he accepted Jesus Christ as his Lord and Savior a few years earlier one Bible passage stood prominently in his heart.

Matt. 28:18-20

And Jesus came and spoke to them, saying, "All authority has been given to Me in heaven and on earth. Go therefore and make disciples of all the nations, baptizing them in the name of the Father, and of the Son and of the Holy Spirit, teaching them to observe all things that I have commanded you; and lo, I am with you always even to the end of the age. Amen

After Livingstone had completed medical school in Glasgow, he heard Robert Moffat, a missionary from Africa. One thing that really stood out for the young Livingstone was 20 words that Moffat spoke. "I have sometimes seen, in the morning sun, the smoke of a thousand villages where no missionary has ever been."

A year after his arrival in Africa, he wrote to his father; "The work of God goes on here notwithstanding all our infirmities. Souls are being gathered continually. Twenty-four were added to the church last month."

Upon his return from a preaching tour, he found that his people had been killed, captured, or driven away by fierce natives of another tribe. As he traveled among the villages, his ox-cart was frequently besieged by crowds of sick, suffering folk, begging the great white doctor to heal them. At night he would sit among the people around the village fire listening to tales of the mighty exploits of ancient heroes. Then he would stand and tell the story of the greatest Hero of all ages, the story of Jesus coming from heaven to earth to die on the Cross. The wonder of Christ's atonement was much in his thinking and in his preaching. One night, while defending the natives against an attack by a wild beast, he broke his finger. Seeing the blood flowing from the injured finger, the people exclaimed: "You saved our lives by wounding yourself. Henceforth our hearts are yours." Telling of the incident in a letter, Livingstone remarked: "I wished that they had felt gratitude for the blood that was shed for their precious souls by Him who was wounded for their transgressions, and had given their hearts to Him."

On his 59th birthday he made this entry in his Journal:

March 19th, birthday. My Jesus, my King, my Life, my All; I again dedicate my whole self to Thee. Accept me and grant, O gracious Father, that ere this year is gone, I may finish my task. In Jesus' name I ask it. Amen, so let it be. David Livingstone.

His all-encompassing objective was to open a way for the heralds of redemption and to apply the Gospel to the task of abolishing the slave trade in the name of Him who said: "The Spirit of the Lord is upon me, because he hath anointed me to preach the gospel ... to preach deliverance to the captives ... and to set at liberty them that are bruised."

In the years that he travelled through Africa, Dr. Livingstone had to contend with hostile tribes, wild animals, slave traders and disease. He followed the path that Jesus had started, and blazed the trail for future missionaries. Upon his death to malaria, the missionary world exploded sending missionaries to the four corners of the world following the path that Jesus had started.

Throughout Africa today, there are many missionary organizations continuing the work that Dr. Livingstone had been called to many years ago. One of these organizations is Far Reaching Ministries.

Thirteen years ago Wes Bentley, founder of FRM, had a vision not of winning one country for God, but for winning the continent of Africa for God. This work is accomplished by training and teaching young men called to ministry, to support combat troops and to spread the Gospel to those people that have never heard of Jesus Christ.

During teaching one day a future group of pastors were being taught Luke 9:23

Then He said to them all, "If anyone desires to come after Me, let him deny himself, and take up his cross daily, and follow Me."

These future pastors took the passage literally and went out and made themselves crosses, which they carry daily. After graduation these pastors frequently found themselves in situations where the troops were outnumbered. With the love of God firmly in their hearts, they would stand up holding their crosses high and begin singing praises to God, all the while bullets whizzing by them. These selfless acts would rally the troops and turn the tide of the battle.

I have tried to show since Jesus Christ was crucified, that Christians would selflessly give of their physical body, for their love of God. With evil lurking around every corner, these Christians would not deviate from the path that God placed before them. Faced with the challenge of death of the flesh or death of the Spirit, I wholeheartedly reply; death of the flesh. How would you reply?

John 5:24

"Most assuredly, I say to you, he who hears My word and believes in Him who sent Me has everlasting life, and shall not come into judgment, but has passed from death into life".

Part II

The Heart of a Servant

*I*f you are worried about the state of your heart; don't worry because at some point in our lives, we all had a hardened heart. There are two distinctive ways our heart can be. We have already discussed the hardened heart. But there is also the heart of a servant, or servant's heart. A servant's heart is someone who walks with God, following the path that God has laid before them; helping their fellow man without looking for any gratification.

At times following God's path isn't an easy one; but when you consider the end result is spending an eternity in God's love, there isn't a better place to be. Most Christians have a combination of a hardened heart and a servant's heart, as they move more on God's path they have more of a servant's heart. There is a constant struggle in our hearts between good and evil, but it is a struggle that is won daily by God's intervention.

A lot of people believe that by attending church, that just by giving up two hours a week to the Lord, that they are saved. The church's role and only role is to guide those who believe by teaching the Scripture; and by leading by example showing non-believers how glorious the love of God is. Salvation is granted by God, and He grants salvation to those who believe and follow Him. Our Lord teaches us what lies ahead when judgment comes

Matthew 7:13-14

Enter by the narrow gate; for wide is the gate and broad is the way that leads to destruction, and there are many who go by in it. Because narrow is the gate and difficult is the way which leads to life, and there are few that find it.

There was one man who unlike the rest of us had a pure servant's heart. It was and is Jesus Christ.

From an early age Jesus Christ knew that He was the sacrificial lamb that would one day bear the sins of mankind on His shoulders, so that man could join God in heaven free of sin. All men faced with the same prospect would cower in the corner and hide, hoping that the sacrifice would not take place. However, Jesus may have been man in physical form, but His heart was something the world had never seen; and the only time the world would see that heart was in Jesus Christ.

Through His ministry the countless lives that He touched, the souls that He saved, is a miracle in its self. There was one miracle that was written about in all four Gospels and that was the feeding of the five thousand.

Mark 6:33-44

But the multitudes saw them departing, and many knew Him and ran there on foot from all the cities. They arrived before them and came together to Him. And Jesus, when He came out, saw a great multitude and was moved with compassion for them, because they were like sheep not having a shepherd. So He began to teach them many things. When the day was now far spent, His disciples came to Him and said "This is a deserted place, and already the hour is late. Send them away, that they may go into the surrounding country and villages and buy themselves bread; for they have nothing to eat. But He answered and said to them "You give them something to eat." And they said to Him "shall we go and buy two hundred denarii worth of bread and give them something to eat?" But He said to them, "how many loaves do you have? Go and see." And when they found out they said "five and two fish." Then He *commanded them to make them all sit down in groups on the green grass. So they sat down in ranks, in hundreds and in fifties. And when He had taken the five loaves and the two fish, He looked up to heaven, blessed and broke the loaves and gave them to His disciples to set before them; and the two fish He divided among them all. So they all ate and were filled. And they took up twelve baskets of fragments and of the fish. Now those who had eaten the loaves were about five thousand men.*

Jesus with a pure servant's heart first administered to their spiritual needs and then He took care of their physical needs by feeding them food. No man is worthy to walk in the Lord's footprints, the best we can do is to walk with the Lord and following the path that has been laid before each of us.

Heart of the Church

When we look at the church; it is a reflection of what is in our hearts. At times the church displays a hardened heart, where it turns away from the laws that God has set forth. Then there are times that the church is full of love for God and follows God's law obediently. However most of the time the church's heart is a combination.

To get better understanding of the church we need to direct our attention to the book of Revelation to get the answer.

Revelation 2:4-5
The loveless church

"Nevertheless I have this against you, that you have left your first love. Remember therefore from where you have fallen; repent and do the first works, or else I will come to you quickly and remove your lampstand from its place, unless you repent."

They must compare their present with their former state, and consider how much better it was with them then, than it is now. How much peace, strength, purity and pleasure they have lost by leaving their first love. How much more cheerful they could awaken in the morning, how much better they could bear afflictions and how much more becomingly they could enjoy the favors of providence How much easier the thoughts of death were to them and how much more stronger their hopes and desires of heaven. They must repent.

Revelation 2:8-10
The persecuted church

"I know your works, tribulation and poverty (but you are rich); and I know the blasphemy of those who say are Jews and are not, but are a synagogue of Satan. Do not fear any of those things which you are about to suffer. Indeed the devil is about to throw some of you into prison, that you may be tested, and you will have tribulation ten days. Be faithful until death, and I will give you the crown of life."

Many, who are rich as to this world, are poor as to the next; and some who are poor outwardly, are inwardly rich; rich in faith, in good works, rich in privileges, rich in gifts, rich in hope. Where there is spiritual plenty, outward poverty may be well borne; and when God's people are made poor as to this life, for the sake of Christ and a good conscience, he makes all up to them in spiritual riches. Christ arms against coming troubles. Fear none of these things; not only forbid slavish fear, but subdue it, furnishing the soul with strength and courage. It should be to try them, not to destroy them. Observe, the sureness of the reward; "I will give thee:" they shall have the reward from Christ's own hand. Also, how suitable it is; "a crown of life:" the life worn out in his service, or laid down in his cause, shall be rewarded with a much better life, which shall be eternal. The second death is unspeakably worse than the first death, both in the agonies of it, and as it is eternal death: it is indeed awful to die, and to be always dying. If a man is kept from the second death and wrath to come, he may patiently endure whatever he meets with in this world.

Revelation 2:14-16

The compromising church

"But I have a few things against you, because you have there, those who hold the doctrine of Balaam, who taught Balak to put a stumbling block before the children of Israel, to eat things sacrificed to idols, and to commit sexual immorality. Thus you also have those who hold the doctrine of Nicolaitans, which thing I hate. Repent, or else I will come to you quickly and will fight against them with the sword of my mouth."

The word of God is a sword, able to slay both sin and sinners. It turns andcuts every way; but the believer need not fear this sword; yet this confidence cannot be supported without steady obedience. As our Lord notices all the advantages and opportunities we have for duty in the places where we dwell, so he notices our temptations and discouragements from the same causes. In a situation of trials, the church of Pergamos had not denied the faith, either by open apostasy, or by giving way so as to avoid the cross.

Christ commends their steadfastness, but reproves their sinful failures. A wrong view of gospel doctrine and Christian liberty was a root of bitterness from which evil practices grew. Repentance is the duty of churches and bodies of men, as well as of particular persons; those who sin together should repent together. Here is the promise of favor to those that overcome. The influences and comforts of the Spirit of Christ come down from heaven into the soul, for its support. This is hidden from the rest of the world. The new name is the name of adoption; when the Holy Spirit shows his own work in the believer's soul, this new name and its real import are understood by him.

Revelation 2:19-23
The corrupt church

"I know your works, your love, service faith, and your patience; and as for your works, the last are more than the first. Nevertheless I have a few things against you, because you allow that woman Jezebel, who calls herself a prophetess, to teach and seduce My servants to commit sexual immorality and to eat things sacrificed to idols. I gave her time to repent of her sexual immorality, but she did not repent. Indeed I will cast her into a sickbed, and those who commit adultery with her into great tribulation, unless they repent of their deeds. And I will kill her children with death, and all the churches shall know that I am He who searches minds and hearts, and I will give to each one of you according to your works."

All Christians should earnestly desire that their last works may be their best works. Yet this church connived at some wicked seducers. God is known by the judgments he executes; and by this upon seducers, he shows his certain knowledge of the hearts of men, of their principles, designs, frame, and temper. Encouragement is given to those who kept themselves pure and undefiled. It is dangerous to despise the mystery of God, and as dangerous to receive the mysteries of Satan. Let us beware of the depths of Satan, of which those who know the least are the most happy. How tender Christ is of his faithful servants! He lays nothing upon his servants but what is for their good. There is promise of an ample reward to the persevering, victorious believer; also knowledge and wisdom, suitable to their power and dominion. Christ brings day with him into the soul, the light of grace and of glory, in the presence and enjoyment of him their Lord and Savior. After every victory let us follow up our advantage against the enemy, that we may overcome and keep the works of Christ to the end.

Revelation 3:1-6
The dead church

"I know your works, that you have a name that you are alive, but you are dead. Be watchful, and strengthen the things which remain, that is ready to die, for I have not found your works perfect before God. Remember therefore how you have received and heard; hold fast and repent. Therefore if you will not watch, I will come upon you as a thief, and you will not know at what hour I will come upon you. You have a few names in Sardis, who have not defiled their garments; and they shall walk with Me in white, for they are worthy. He who overcomes shall be clothed in white garments, and I will not blot out his name from the Book of Life; but I will confess his name before My Father and before His angels. He, who has an ear, let him hear what the Spirit says to the churches."

Unbelievers, those whose names are not written in the book of life, will be judged solely because of their works. Outwardly this church has the façade of being believers; but when you take a close look at this church, it is so steeped in traditions that the word of God is lost. The congregation goes through the motions of a faithful practicing church, but there is no dimension to their faith.

Revelation 3:8-13
The faithful church

"I know your works. See, I have set before you an open door, and no one can shut it; for that you have a little strength, have kept My word, and have not denied My name. Indeed, I will make those of the synagogue of Satan who say that they are Jews and are not, but lie—indeed, I will make them come and worship before your feet, and to know that I have loved you. Because you have kept My command to persevere, I also will keep you from the hour of trial which shall come upon the whole world, to test those who dwell on the earth. I am coming quickly! Hold fast what you have, that no one may take your crown. He who overcomes, I will make him a pillar in the temple of My God, and he shall go out no more. I will write on him the name of my God and the name of the city of My God, the New

Jerusalem, which comes down out of heaven from my God. And I will write on him My new name. He, who has an ear, let him hear what the Spirit says to the churches."

Although Christ accepts a little strength, yet believers must not rest satisfied in a little, but strive to grow in grace, to be strong in faith, giving glory to God. Christ can discover this favor to his people, so that their enemies shall be forced to acknowledge it. This, by the grace of Christ, will soften their enemies, and make them desire to be admitted into communion with his people. Christ promises preserving grace in the most trying times, as the reward of past faithfulness; To him that hath shall be given. Those who keep the gospel in a time of peace shall be kept by Christ in an hour of temptation; and the same Divine grace that has made them fruitful in times of peace, will make them faithful in times of persecution. Christ promises a glorious reward to the victorious believer. He shall be a monumental pillar in the temple of God; a monument of the free and powerful grace of God; a monument that shall never be defaced or removed. On this pillar shall be written the new name of Christ; by this will appear, under whom the believer fought the good fight, and came off victorious.

Revelation 3:15-22
The lukewarm church

"I know your works, that you are neither cold nor hot. I could wish you were cold or hot. So then, because you are lukewarm, and neither cold nor hot, I will vomit you out of my mouth. Because you say, "I am rich; I have become wealthy, and have need of nothing"—and do not know that you are wretched, miserable, poor, blind, and naked. I counsel you to buy from Me gold refined in the fire, that you may be rich; and white garments, that you may be clothed, that the shame of your nakedness may not be revealed ; and anoint your eyes with eye salve, that you may see. As many as I love, I rebuke and chasten. Therefore be zealous and repent. Behold, I stand at the door and knock. If any one hears my voice and opens the door, I will come in to him and dine with him, and he with Me. To him who overcomes, I will grant to sit with Me on My throne, as I also overcame and sat down with My Father on Hs throne. He, who has an ear, let him hear what the Spirit says to the churches."

If religion is worth anything, it is worth everything. Christ expects men should be in earnest. How many professors of gospel doctrine are neither hot nor cold; except as they are indifferent in needful matters, and hot and fiery in disputes about things of lesser moment! A severe punishment is threatened. They would give a false opinion of Christianity, as if it were an unholy religion; while others would conclude it could afford no real satisfaction, otherwise its professors would not have been heartless in it, or so ready to seek pleasure or happiness from the world. One cause of this indifference and inconsistency in religion is, self-conceit and self-delusion; "Because thou sayest." What a difference between their thoughts of themselves, and the thoughts Christ had of them! How careful should we be not to cheat our own souls! There are many in hell, who once thought themselves far in the way to heaven. Let us beg of God that we may not be left to flatter and deceive ourselves. Professors grow proud, as they become carnal and formal. Their state was wretched in itself. They were poor; really poor, when they said and thought they were rich. They could not see their state, nor their way, nor their danger, yet they thought they saw it. They had not the garment of justification, nor sanctification: they were exposed to sin and shame; their rags that would defile them. They were naked, without house or harbor, for they were without God, in whom alone the soul of man can find rest and safety. Good counsel was given by Christ to this sinful people. Happy those who take his counsel, for all others must perish in their sins. Christ lets them know where they might have true riches, and how they might have them. Some things must be parted with, but nothing valuable; and it is only to make room for receiving true riches. Part with sin and self-confidence, that you may be filled with his hidden treasure. They must receive from Christ the white raiment he purchased and provided for them; his own imputed righteousness for justification, and the garments of holiness and sanctification. Let them give themselves up to his word and Spirit, and their eyes shall be opened to see their way and their end. Let us examine ourselves by the rule of his word, and pray earnestly for the teaching of his Holy Spirit, to take away our pride, prejudices, and worldly lusts. Sinners ought to take the rebukes of God's word and rod, as tokens of his love to their souls. Christ stood without; knocking, by the dealings of his providence, the warnings and teaching of his word, and the influences of his Spirit. Christ still graciously, by his word and Spirit, comes to the door of the hearts of sinners. Those who open to him shall enjoy his presence. If what he finds would make but a poor feast, what he brings will supply a rich one. He will give fresh supplies of graces and comforts. In the conclusion is a promise to the overcoming believer. Christ himself had temptations and conflicts; he overcame them all, and was more than a conqueror. Those made like to Christ in his trials, shall be made like to him in glory. All is closed with the general demand of attention. And these counsels, while suited to the churches to which they were addressed, are deeply interesting to all men.

What Jesus has taught us about the seven churches is that He is referring to seven conditions of man's heart. Looking at the seven churches in a different light; the faithful and persecuted churches were the only ones not rebuked by Jesus, these would be the servant's heart. The remaining five; dead, compromising, lukewarm, corrupt and loveless churches is referring to the hardened heart of man.

This can also be viewed as different levels of love towards God.

Hardened heart
- Lukewarm
- Compromising
- Corrupt
- Loveless
- Dead

With a lukewarm heart, your heart is in a condition where your heart is hot and cold towards God. When in this state generally you turn to God in times of trouble, when you think the world is coming to an end, or you are involved with something in your life that you have no control over and don't know how to deal with it. The rest of the time you ignore calls from God, and live life for yourself. In this condition you are on the edge between salvation and an eternity of damnation in the fires of hell. Unfortunately in today's society this is the most prevalent heart condition. For most of my adult life this was the condition that my heart was in, but I reached out to God repented for my sins, gave Him my heart, he reached His hand out to me and saved me. If you don't repent and give God your heart, you will begin the perilous fall to the gates of hell.

Your heart will go through a transition into the

compromising stage. At this point you will begin to compromise your Godly values for your own worldly pleasures. What was important to you before will now have less prominence. The image of God will begin to blur and fade as you take your focus off of Him

If you haven't repented yet, your journey continues; you have forgotten or don't believe that Jesus died for your sins, and was raised on the third day and sits on the right hand of God to judge the living and the dead. Your heart is now corrupted, where your focus is firmly on yourself and it doesn't matter to you if you take advantage of brothers and sisters in Christ.

Perhaps you once believed in God, asked God for intervention in a particular matter, and it wasn't answered or wasn't the answer you were seeking. God answers all prayers but in may not be when we seek the answer, or the answer we seek. Remember growing up and asking your dad for something, it wasn't always the answer or the time that we wanted, but our dad didn't love us any less. You didn't always agree with the decision so what you asked, you may have done anyway regardless of the circumstances. It is the same way when we ask God something. You have turned away from God, your heart has no love for God, and you don't listen to God or respond to His touch.

If you still haven't repented and given your life to God, you are now standing before the gates of hell with a dead heart. You never had a relationship with God, or even took to trouble to get to know Him. You probably have the thought "who cares, I had fun." But you have no one to share it with, you are all alone; no family, no friends. Nothing just an eternity by yourself in the lake of fire and brimstone; doesn't that sound pleasant.

If you are in any of these stages and are despairing about where you are headed; God is listening. When you repent and give yourself to God, He will be there to save you, it's not too late.

That is the state of five of the churches or states of man's heart, but there are two left that are beacons to God's love, the persecuted church and the faithful church.

With a persecuted heart, you have a heart that is so in love with God that regardless of the circumstances your love for God doesn't waiver. With a persecuted heart if you were put into a situation where you could deny God to save your life, or have your life taken for your belief in God; a persecuted believer would freely and openly give their physical life for eternal life with God. The world today is full of people that have never known the glory or felt the love of God. Organizations like Far Reaching Ministries to name one are bringing the love of God, to those who don't yet have a relationship with God. They are being persecuted on a daily basis by groups that don't understand the faith in God that they have. Missionary organizations do this globally because the message of God must be shared with everyone. Missionaries are being tortured and killed for their faith in God, to these blessed groups to sacrifice their mortal lives; to bring unbelievers to the love of God is a small price to play.

A faithful heart is very similar to a persecuted, but it is different. A believer with a faithful heart will willingly do anything that God asks of them regardless of the circumstances. A hero that saves life is a good example of having a faithful heart.

We all have someone we look up to because of a heroic act. In my life the one I look up to is my granddad Hugh Ritchie. I have never known the joy of spending time with him; God called him home when my dad was three, but through my dad's wisdom and love for others, my granddad lives through him.

From the eastern Scottish village of Gourdon, at a young age he became a fisherman. During one of his fishing trips a rogue wave hit the fishing boat knocking a crewmate overboard. With a history of seafaring in his blood, swimming was second nature to granddad. The crewmate continued to flounder in the rough seas, granddad jumped in to save his life. Today most fishermen are trained in CPR, but in those days very few were trained, fortunately my granddad was trained. The crewmate's life was saved that day partially due to the actions of granddad, but more for his love of God. Granddad was awarded the Stanhope Medal for bravery and the Carnegie trust, because of his actions that day. If I had been able to talk to granddad about the experience, I am sure from what I have learned from my dad, granddad would have made little of the whole thing; that he did it because someone was in trouble.

Some churches today have a faithful heart; When you think of motorsports, you have the image of speed and a carefree lifestyle. There was a void that needed to be filled, and in 1971, a small group of godly men from Southern California tried to fill that void when they started Racers For Christ (RFC).

Motorsports take place on the weekend, when most people have the weekend off. With 75 million Americans attending motorsports events, there was no time for the participants to attend a traditional Sunday church service.

That is one of the blessings that RFC brings to motorsports. Before a race begins, RFC chaplains conduct church services right there at the track. These are non-denominational services where everyone is invited to attend. When you attend an RFC chapel service, you'll see racers who will later in the day be competing against each other sitting together sharing the love of God as brothers and sisters.

When you look into your heart to understand what type of heart you have, also think about selfless acts that you have done, not for your glory but for the glory of God. Maybe you have helped the homeless by helping out those less fortunate. It might be when you smile at someone and offer a comforting word to help someone through their day. These are all examples of selfless acts. These are all acts that Jesus Christ did on a daily basis.

Conclusion

I have challenge for you, and the challenge is also for me. I know how easy it is to be overcome by sin. Keep God in the center of everything you do. Learn God's love through His grace and love for His creation by studying His word. The Bible didn't end two thousand years ago but it continues to grow in each of us who profess our faith and love of God. Make it part of your journey. Each day millions of people around the world give their lives to God; are you one of them? This book has been a journey to expose not only the greed of man, but the greed of this man. But the book doesn't end here. The journey continues. The journey won't end till we stand before the Lord and He says "Good Job (your name here) my faithful servant. I hope and pray that no one stands before the Lord and the Lord says "who are you? I don't know you" Jesus gave his life for us; are you prepared to do the same for Jesus?

Deliverance

Heavenly Father I fall to my knees in praise for the glory of Your love;
When I was shrouded in darkness and alone, You fought the battle with Satan and brought me into the light and glory of Your love.
God has heard my pleas for help, and answered with resounding glory that shook the world as one of Your lambs have been saved.
Halleluiah!! To God the Father Almighty!!
The wolves of evil have Your flock surrounded, patiently waiting for their moment to strike.
God Help us, the wolves are running towards us!!
Our Shepherd is needed to strike fear into the hearts of the wolves.
Behold our Shepherd is coming, on a white horse His eyes are like the flames of fire.
Watch out! Wolves, your time is near, judgment is upon you.
O God, Father Almighty, we fall to our knees in praise for deliverance from the wolves.
Halleluiah!! Our Shepherd, our Savior, the light of creation.
Amen

Conclusion

Luke 9:23

Then He said to them all, "If anyone desires to come after Me, let him deny himself, take up his cross daily and follow Me.

PLEASE DON'T BE THE PERSON THAT JESUS DOESN'T KNOW

References

NKJV Study Bible (2007) Thomas Nelson, Nashville

Jacobus de Voragine The Golden Legend (2002) Medival Source Book

Jewish Virtual Library

Far Reaching Ministries

Racers for Christ

Henry Matthew Commentary of the whole Bible (2008) Henrickson Peabody

www.ingramcontent.com/pod-product-compliance
Ingram Content Group UK Ltd.
Pitfield, Milton Keynes, MK11 3LW, UK
UKHW022222230426
12048UKWH00016BA/1014